Poems from

Essex & Elsewhere

Poems from Essex & Elsewhere

McClain Jeffrey Moredock

Essex Editions

Poems from Essex & Elsewhere
Copyright © 2016 by McClain Jeffrey Moredock
Cover design by Essex Editions
Book design by Katie Shepard

All rights reserved. No part of this book may be reproduced or transmitted in any form or by any means, electronic or mechanical, including photocopying, recording or by any information storage and retrieval system, without written permission from the publisher, except for the inclusion of brief quotations in a review.

Published in the United States by Essex Editions.

ISBN-10:0-9967870-4-6
ISBN-13:978-0-9967870-4-8

Essex Editions
Post Office Box 25
Essex, New York 12936
www.essexeditions.com
contact@essexeditions.com

For Etta and our children and grandchildren

CONTENTS

POEMS FROM ESSEX

INTRODUCTION 1
It Takes All Kinds to Raise a Village 7
Excess Day in the Village of Essex 9
A Ferry Tale 11
The 4th of July Parade 14
On the Porch 17
If A Tree Falls in the Woods, Does Anyone Care? 18
Snapshots 19
The 501 Year Old Man of Essex 22
The Archbishop of Essex, A Woman For All Seasons 27
Down the Hill, Over the River, Up the Hill 29
Political Speech 31
The Essex Winter of 2011-12 32

POEMS FROM ELSEWHERE

INTRODUCTION 39
Whether Report 40
Reflecting on the Demolition of Lock #6 On the
Monongahela River 41
Global Warning 44
The Intruder 46
The Faculty Meeting (collegium militari) 48
Frank Stella's Darabjerd III 49

The Third Law of Theodynamics	50
The Guitarist	51
A Fracking Shame	52
Punkuation	53
Stoned	54
Thought For Food	55
The Critics	56
Christmas Eve	57
Merry Crispness	58
A Christmas Cheer	59
Rock Music	60
Paradise Remembered	61
Ipso Facto	63
The Ascension	64
Right Now	65
Gawf	66
Imitation of Christ	67
The Secret of the Golden Trout	69
Last Standing Man	71
You've Got to Give to Get	72
On Celebrating My 77th Birthday	74
ABOUT THE AUTHOR	75

INTRODUCTION

The twelve poems in the first part of this slim volume are all set in and around Essex, New York, a small village on the western shore of Lake Champlain. It is one of two ports to a ferry that runs back and forth between New York and Vermont. The trip takes 20 to 30 minutes during which passengers can enjoy the Green Mountains to the east, the Adirondacks to west, and 125 miles of blue water stretched from north to south. Essex is a place where many people stop on their way to somewhere else, but I believe very few are one-time visitors.

In 1980 my family and I became summer residents in Essex when a local realtor residing above the post office found us a house just south of the village. When all the papers were signed and we were the happy owners of Windy Hill, she said, "You know, this summer Essex is really going to take off!" Over 37 years later, the village is still idling on the runway. Most would say, "Thank God for that!"

These poems were written with great affection and deep appreciation for our seasonal life along the Adirondack Coast. Here's to Essex, The Gem of the Adirondack Coast!

* * *

Over the last forty years my writing has included sermons, articles, letters to the editor, a collection of short stories, a half-finished novel, and close to a 100 poems. Many of the latter have been celebratory pieces for family and friends noting birthdays, weddings, and childbirths. The remaining poetry and occasional prose have been efforts to mine irony ore from the daily news.

I love words. I love playing with words. Most of all I love employing words to provide an unfamiliar perspective. On occasion, others see things the way I do. When they don't, I appreciate discovering a new point of view.

Essex

It Takes All Kinds to Raise a Village

Two roads, a ferry, and a lake
Do not a city make
Nor hamlet so I read
For hamlets have no churches
Nor government to lead

But the lovely intersection
Of travel wet and dry
Are perfect for the village
That lives in my mind's eye

Now those who visit, those who stay
Are not quite all the same
Each has its own perspective
Each sings its own refrain

The village has old timers
And latecomers in its fold
Plus an influx of summer folks
Who leave when it gets cold

Now toss in all the travelers
Who are only passing through
Some stop and have a bite to eat
And all enjoy the view

This mixture of humanity
Creates a potpourri
Which means within the village
People often disagree

Of course they hate the winter
And warmly welcome summer
But when it comes to politics
Its glum and even glummer

No unifying vision
No common cause for all
But rather each to owns the cry
On Main Street or Town Hall

But the village seems to thrive
And remain a lakeside treasure
For residents and visitors
All love it in full measure

June 2015

Excess Day in the Village of Essex

On the eve of Excess Day
Husbands and wives
Can be heard
Bickering back and forth
Trying to determine whose excess
Must leave the house

Husbands cling to old rods and reels
Wives insist they need their curling irons
Small children hide balls and dolls
They haven't played with for years
Dogs hide their worn-out chew toys

When dawn breaks on Excess Day
The sidewalks are lined with the
Detritus of daily life
Fishing reels curling irons balls
And dolls and much much more

Crowds sweep down the street
In search of bargains treasures or
Just something they don't have
And don't need or so say
Husbands to wives
And wives to husbands

By mid-day prices begin to drop
As the throngs begin to thin
Books birdhouses bar stools
Pottery paintings and more

Fly off the sidewalks and
Before long the day is ended

One family's excess is now another
Family's excess and sure to be seen
Next year on the
Other side of the street

June 2013

A Ferry Tale

I await the sound
Of snapping synapse
On a singular sunny day
When a captain,
A regular sort by all reports,
Sings out to no one in particular
I've had it!
And the Henry Aiken slowly turns,
Not south to Whitehall but
North toward Montreal
Heading for a foreign shore
A snap decision
Made by one for many
The passengers…
The drivers, the walk-ons, the cyclists
See two distant shores
Maintain their distance

An elderly couple from Canada
Their first ferry ride
Three texting teens from Teaneck
All bruised from college interviews
A family of six from Secaucus
Cuddle in a camper bearing a sticker
That says *FURTHER!*
Ten walk-ons and four cyclists
All left in one state
Expecting to be in another

But the Henry Aiken chugs on
Heading north

The captain bolts
The pilothouse door.
A crew member pounds and shouts
Fruitless
He sees his captain,
Beatific look and all
Staring due north

Finally a din from the deck
Passengers sing out in alarm
A chorus of complaints
Supplicating arms wave in the wind
Walkers and drivers and bikers
Realize their lives have changed course
Of course but to where
They do not know

"Stop!"
"Turn around!"
"Take me to shore, any shore"
Tensions mount, dismount, then remount
The captive chorus swells off-key

But then there is a lull and a few
A very few begin a new song
A song of liberation a song
Of great adventure
No more back and forth
But where?

Eight hours later the ferry
Comes to a narrow canal
Drained of diesel and desire

It stops and sits
But an addendum looms
One more act
A final reckoning
The captain is fired
Then rehired
Thanks to a Free Press

For the passengers
Almost to a person have
Swallowed their anger
Dropped their suits and
Forever will tell anyone
Who will listen
"For one whole day
We all felt just like Robert Frost"

August 2011

The 4th of July Parade

It comes to life
In the shadow of St. Phillip.
Wayne Baily, a real trooper,
Calms the restless crowd
With a litany of, *"Soon"*,
"Any minute now", and
"Almost here", then
A salvo of comments
About passers-by who
Catch his eye… and then… when
The crowd has worked itself
Into what passes for a frenzy
In Essex, New York,
It rumbles into view!
Ignoring the blinking red light,
It fills the street.
Convertibles piled high with
Politicians,
Floats awash in small children,
A small armada of ancient tractors
Carry a small army of ancient farmers,
Candy flies through the air,
Ignoble savages from Reber in red face
(And in need of dentures)
Run from side to side,
Frighten small children,
Try to grope large women.
A fire truck rolls past.
More candy flies through the air;
Bag pipes and drums march by.
Cats scream to get out of their bags;
Chests resonate.

A unicyclist wobbles along
Juggling cucumbers.
A vintage car glides by,
Vintage owner looking smug.
Another fire truck
Deafens ears with a blast.
The sheriff passes, riding high
In the back seat,
(Not his usual place).
A hazmat truck slides by, and
Suddenly, we feel less safe.
Yet another fire truck.
More candy flies by.
Water cannons dampen our
Enthusiasm, but we recover quickly
And… when the excitement
Becomes almost unbearable,
It all ends.

Many want it to come again
And it did one lean year
When it doubled back
For a second run.
But not this year.
Church ladies still hawk
Strawberry shortcake.
Fire Department volunteers
Push hot dogs.
One Essex citizen sells
Helium-filled balloons
For a good cause,
But most escape their

Owners and head
Out of town.
Children have bulging cheeks and
Bags of airborne candy.
A man from Willsboro claims,
To anyone who will listen,
That he was struck in the eye
By a wayward Tootsie Roll.
He gets smiles but no sympathy.
Trooper Baily thanks a few dozen people
And we all head home.
Grateful that our nation
Has had another birthday.

August 2011

On the Porch

to sit and see
day or night
to catch light's play
from sun or moon
on cloud or water
is to look within
and know… again
we live by grace
and grace alone

2014

If A Tree Falls in the Woods, Does Anyone Care?

I thought that I would never see
A poem as lovely as a tree
But then a watery blue did make
A view serene that made me take
A point of view set on a lake

But o'er the years the trees did grow
As I watched my lake view slowly go
First the lake and then far shore
Soon Camel's Hump will be no more

No longer do I love all trees
Especially those that do not please
Growing up to make a screen
A wall of wood, a scrim of green

So now I say grab saw and axe
Let's give them all a few good whacks
And to those known as Tree Huggers
I say move over for Tree Muggers

August 19, 2015

Snapshots

History Lesson
A man who was called de'Champlain
Said life here in France tres mundane
A long journey I'll take
Perhaps discover a lake
Which someday may bear my name

Town Bulletin Board
A colorful mosaic of
Opportunity and desire.

Begg's Point Playground
Where have all the
Children gone?

Essex Post Office
Who says the feds
Can't do
Anything right?

The Essex Inn
She's not her
Old self.
Thank God!

Red Light District
No hookers or hustlers
At 22 and Main,
But temptation lurks

On every corner
Politics, Religion, Art,
And ice cream.

The Old Dock
Order a brew.
Enjoy the view.
Skip the stew.

Lake Champlain Yoga & Wellness
Harold Tart would
Be pleased that people
In his old store
Can still
Get worked over.

The Essex Marina
On occasion,
The only submarine base
On Lake Champlain.

Renew Shop
The perfect place
For those who
Have too much and…
Those who don't have enough.

Brass House
It disappeared
Behind a curtain of
Oxidation.

Wand & Wade
They play a game of
Wood, paper, and paint.
One goes for humor,
The other for quaint.

The DNC
The Do-Nothing Club got its fame
By being so true to its name.
Men drink coffee and talk,
Trading bards as they squawk.
The agenda is always the same.

ECHO
People love hearing
The sound of
Their own voice.

The Crater Club
John Burnam built a retreat
Where the elite could meet, drink, and eat.
He called the club Crater,
But it should be called Critter
For the wildlife think it's quite neat.

Over Many Years

The 501 Year Old Man of Essex
with apologies to Mel and Carl

"I'm standing here today with a man who claims to have lived in the village of Essex for 500 years."

"Excuse me, I said 501 years. I had a birthday last Tuesday."

"Okay, 501. That's a lot of years to spend in one place."

"You're telling me. About 200 years ago I took a day trip to Port Henry, and decided I might as well just stay at home. I haven't left since."

"I guess what puzzles me is that you claim to have lived in Essex for 501 years, but the sign on the edge of town says Essex was founded in 1785, and that's only 230 years ago."

"Founded? Founded? That's the word they use to describe what a bunch of latecomers claim. Started to show up from down state in New Amsterdam that year and claimed to have 'found' our village. Actually, we 'found' them wandering around looking for a place to eat and property to buy."

"Now, let's go back to then."

"Yes, let's go back to then now."

"I want to know what it was like in those very early days."

"Well, it was pretty quiet. Some days you could hear the dogs snoring as they slept in the street."

"Wow, that's quiet."

"Yes, and sometimes they didn't even snore."

"I'm curious; there must have been some Native Americans in the area."

"Of course. *We* were the Native Americans."

"No, I mean the savages who painted their faces and wore loincloths."

"Oh, the Indians. Sure, they were all around us."

"You called them Indians?"

"No, that's what they called themselves. Claimed to have moved here. Come all the way from Indiana."

"Were they hostile?"

"No, mostly Iroquois, a few Mohawk, and the odd Ottawa."

"No, no, I mean were they aggressive toward the people in the village."

"No, not at all. They smoked a lot of a weedy grass they cultivated, and it seemed to make them very placid and giggly. It also made them hungry. They were always coming into town to get something to eat."

"Apart from the Indians, did the village have any other visitors back then?"

"Well, yes, first we had a wave of Frenchies who passed through. Mostly, they were looking for animal pelts, and to tell the truth, they smelled like animal pelts. They did leave us with some good wine and taught us how to fry potatoes, but otherwise, they were pretty unmemorable."

"Did the British ever come by?"

"Come by? Come by? I'll say. Not only did they come by, a whole bunch of them stayed. How do you think places like Port Henry, Willsboro, and Elizabethtown got their names? The British were fascinated with all that monarchy stuff, and god, did they ever love to have a tea party. Damn dull affairs if you ask me. They would sit around complaining about the weather and the local government while downing gallons of tea. We called them the Tea Party People. One local guy referred to them as the Pee Tardy People, kind of an inside joke…"

"Was there much of a social scene?"

"Oh, sure. We had dances, quilting bees, bingo, and frequent Champlains."

"Champlains?"

"Yes, they were gatherings for educational improvement. We would hear a lecture on local flora and fauna, listen to a poet, or even have a mock debate about taxes. People would travel all the way from Reber to join in."

"So, it sounds like there was a lot going on."

"Yes, Essex was a hot bed of literary and political discourse."

"Really, an active political scene?"

"Oh, yes, especially in the competition between men and women for leadership roles. A lot of the men thought a woman's place was in a flowerbed or a kitchen, not in the town hall. But we always had a secret ballot, and women had the votes."

"What a time to be in Essex. Politics, culture, Indians, French, British…"

"For sure. And Essex enjoyed a steady stream of visitors who would canoe across the lake for the day when the weather was agreeable. They never stayed overnight, as most were dairy farmers and had to get back to their herds. But, the people who really had an impact were the Sunbirds."

"Sunbirds?"

"Yep, Sunbirds. People would travel to Essex from other parts of the country to relax and recreate during the summer."

"These Sunbirds, what were they like?"

"Well, they were all pretty well to do. Dressed all natty-like, ate out a lot, and they sure could drink. A whole flock of 'em hung out together just south of town in a place they called The Critter Club."

"The Critter Club? Odd name."

"Not really, every summer when they arrived they would have to kick out all the critters that had spent the winter in their places, called 'em camps. Course, they'd move back in soon as the Sunbirds headed south for the winter. Sort of a joint tenancy kind of arrangement."

"Were there any special activities in Essex?"

"Well, I don't know about special, but there were annual events that everyone looked forward to."

"Tell me about some of them."

"We always had a big parade on the 4th of July."

"Wait a minute, this was long before the war for independence and all that."

"Sure was, funny how the nation's birthday ended up being the same day we celebrated the end of winter."

"The end of winter on July 4th?"

"Yep, it was usually over by then. Winters were long and hard back then. Freezes in June, frosts in July, and sometimes the ice would have just gone out of the lake when it was time for the parade. We don't have winters like that anymore, so it's a good thing our nation got born on that day."

"Were there any other special events?"

"One of my favorites still goes on, Excess Day."

"Excess Day? Is that like Leap Year?"

"Oh, no, it happened every year during the dog days of August. Everyone in town would go through their possessions and put everything they had too much of out on the sidewalk the night before Excess Day. Then, the next day, folks would stroll up and down Main Street buying things they didn't have enough of. Course, the next year a lot of the stuff they bought would end up in front of their house for sale. Fortunately, people came from other towns on Excess Day and bought stuff, so the total excess did diminish a bit from year to year."

"Well, you certainly describe a colorful village lifestyle."

"Sure is, especially in the fall when the leaves turn. Winter's a bit black and white, but spring gets green, and summer's a riot. As for lifestyle, I don't know how stylish we are, but in Essex life is good, very good..."

Summer 2013

The Archbishop of Essex, A Woman For All Seasons

St. John's By the Lake was in need of a priest.
So they cast their net widely, north, west, south, and east.

But what they hauled in wasn't so hot,
A mixed catch at best, the whole vestry thought.

Some were too young, some were too old,
Some wanted city, most couldn't stand cold.

But then when the search looked like it would fail
A grace filled folder arrived in the mail.

A curriculum vitae proclaiming good news.
At last St. John's might have someone to choose!

The Vestry cried out, "She could be our new rector
Let's invite her to Essex so we can inspect her!"

Her initial impression lifted St John's depression.
"A match made in heaven," was the all round expression.

Her first name was Margaret, her last name was Shaw,
Her theology simple, based on love and not law.

Her pastoral style was never a role.
She was always herself, an authentic soul.

SNAFUS were handled so well at the altar
That even God's judgment never could fault her.

So five years flew by and St. John's grew stronger,
As the line for communion got longer and longer.

But all good things finally come to a close
And the good Rev. Margie said, "I need some repose."

St. John's shed a tear; there was not a dry eye.
But then in one voice the members did cry

We'll miss you Margie for hundreds of reasons
The best rector we've had for all of our seasons

Thank you, thank you, thank you indeed
For loving us all,
Bon voyage, safe travels,
and, of course, God speed.

From all the St. John's Sinners and Winners, 2014

Down the Hill, Over the River, Up the Hill

As you drive north on Route 22
Don't drive too fast, but enjoy the view

Wildflower field and trees galore
Rock walls, lake views, and much much more

Then voila', you're in Willsboro
Look all around, be sure to be thorough

A village of the sort one might forget
As it sits and straddles the river Boquet

But it has stores, real entrepreneurs,
One with unbeaten meat and full cans of Coors

It has gravel and stone for sale by the ton
Once sold by the father, now sold by the son

There's even a local Tower of Babel
Known to all who subscribe as TV by cable

There's antiques and junque, and items quite used
Many quite tired, a few look abused

For a work-out drop in at Noblewood Park
You can swim all day, and drink until dark

Or tennis courts that are open to all
But alas no toilet if you hear nature's call

And golf, of course, on the road to The Point
The holes test your skill, the terrain every joint

Restaurants are many, some good, some okay
But all offer drinks, it's The North Country Way

But to really commit a gastronomical sin
Have a Michigan (buried) at the Dew Drop Inn

Or to feed the mind, make a real knowledge gain
Take an hour or two to visit the Paine

There's a museum too with views of the past
And a center for seniors, all good to the last

So that's Willsboro, with a Point and a Heights
But nothing is better than one of its sights

It's the river that flows all the way to Champlain
And like all rivers, it's never the same

Ice in the winter, flooding in spring
In summer and fall, it has beauty to bring

So Willsboro has no need for regret
For its greatest treasure is the river Boquet

July 13, 2015

Political Speech

I blah blah blah America blah blah blah freedom bladdy blah red blah white blah blue blah religion yeah founding fathers ranana ranana motherhood etcetera the flag yak yak yak illegal aliens boo hiss taxes cut cut cut gay marriage yuck the Constitution yada yada yada promise promise promise Washington no no no apple pie yum

2013

The Essex Winter of 2011-12

The Old Man is back!
The Old Man is back!
He does not enter on temperate tiptoes.
Noooooo!
He stomps in from high peaks
Wearing hob-nailed boots.
He crushes the last foolish flower,
Kicks away all memories of leafy color.
Beats at doors, raps on windows,
Freezes fingers, nips noses.
The Old Man is back!

We adjust gradually, swaddled in down,
Mittened, gloved, scarved, mufflered,
The less hardy, balaclavaed.
We talk of witch's breasts, and
Well digger's buttocks.

With the curtain still up on Act One,
Act Two opens on the same stage.
Sheet after sheet of bright white percale
Floats down from above.
It is the monstrous mother
Of all January White Sales.
Sheets pile up and up and up.
The Hawk spreads his windy wings,
Bares his talons, swoops to and fro,
Screams in our ears, tears at our clothes.

It goes on and on and on and on and on and on.
The Green Mountains are still across the lake,
But the White Mountains, once far away,

Now loom large in our yards,
On porches, along driveways.
Roads disappear cars refuse to leave garages.
School buses sit idle and empty.
Children and teachers rejoice.
Mothers and fathers weep silently.
The whether or not man lies again and again,
Tells us a break is in sight,
But he is in a warm studio looking at a camera.
We are in cold houses staring at frosted windows.

Then it happens, *mirabile dictu!*
The sun, for many arctic moons a stranger,
Appears in the sky and beams down.
Adults go outside and smile.
Small children say, "Mommy, Mommy,
What's that shiny ball in the sky?"
We laugh, confident that we will survive.
We wax skis, order snowshoes from L.L. Bean,
Talk a great deal about exercise.
But, alas, a heavy gray cloud cover
Draws itself over the percale.
Everyone goes back inside
To read, to wait, and to drink.

Eternity downshifts into low gear.
We shovel, we scrape, we slip, we slide,
And—when cabin fever
Approaches epidemic proportions—
A change springs into view.
Our world warms.
The percale is peeled away one sheet at a time.

Hearts and minds and ponds begin to thaw.
A few small white mountains remain,
But now there are green valleys to walk through.
Children and teachers are back in school.
Mothers and fathers rejoice.

As Act Two slowly fades from view
Act Three rumbles onto center stage.
It offers a light and sound show.
Some remember Woodstock,
But spirits dampen and droop
From downpour after downpour.
Moss grows between our toes.
Goldie's locks fall straight.
Even non-believers walk on water.
There is talk of ark building.
A baby is born. He is named Noah.
He thrives, but the downpour continues.

At last the gods grow weary of their sport
The big spigot goes righty-tighty
And we see… dry land.
The primal fluid that poured into our lives
Now gushes and rushes down rivers and streams
Until it ends where it always ends,
At the lake's edge
An edge now closer than ever before,
Or so we are told.

Large chunks of lakefront real estate
Disappear into a muddy miasma.
Owners wonder, "Will my taxes go down
Because I now own less land?
Or will they go up now that I am closer to the lake?"

The Wise Guys of Whallonsburg opine
They will go up. They always go up.

The lake heads west, engulfs the ferry landing.
Tourism and interstate commerce tread water.
The Old Dock is too old to move to higher ground.
The marinas are afloat without a boat.
The Rudder Club loses its liquor license,
Again.

Act Three appears endless,
But there is a plan.
Allah be praised; salvation's at hand.
We awake one fine morning
And dress in our t-shirts and shorts.
The percale sheets have drifted away.
No primal fluid drips from the sky.
The edge of the lake creeps east.
The most divine of plans is at hand.
Just when we had thought
We could no longer endure
Another minute of The Old Man,
The Hawk, the Piles of Percale,
Pelting Primal Fluid, and a lake
That didn't know its right place,
The God With Many Names gives us…
Summer!

May 2011

Elsewhere

INTRODUCTION

Early human history is divided into Stone, Bronze, and Iron Ages. Based on more recent history, we have been living for some time in the Age of Irony. How else to explain the apparent incongruity between expectation and actuality? The Paleolithic and Neolithic are long past, and we are well into what might be called the Neo-emetic. However, I believe in the recoverability if not the perfectibility of man, and I hope the following poems reflect my guarded optimism. Written over a span of forty years, they are the result of experience filtered through free association, leavened by faith. As a cancer survivor, I treat each new day as a gift, and welcome its offering of what William Saroyan called "the human comedy." My family and my faith are inseparable, and to write is to live.

Whether Report

Early mourning clouds
Will hang heavy
Between head and heart
Followed by
Teardrop drizzle causing
Limited visibility and
Topical depression

By mid-day winds of change
And sunshine smile
Will allow gradual clearing
Between head and heart
Followed by a warming trend
Probability of participation 100%

March 1975

Reflecting on the Demolition of Lock #6 On the Monongahela River

From my back porch I watched
Lifting and lowering of
Barges emptied then
Filled with coal
West Virginia hollow to
Great gaping mill mouths in
Pittsburgh

I heard the whistle of
The John Zubeck
One of many with
Its high-pitched knock
On your great gates
And then your answer
A whistle low
From deep within
Your concrete chest

With a boat locked tight
In your embrace
Its crew would come ashore
To buy
Prince Albert (in a tin)
Ritz Crackers (in a box)
And then at
Remo's Beer Garden
Iron City (in a bottle)
All that water
Must have made them thirsty

I never could get close to you
From fear of Axis sabotage
And no Jack Armstrong
In our town
A high wire fence
Kept us all away
But still we watched

When sending forth
From your embrace
A boat upstream
My friends and I
Would yell
Hey Cook
And hope to get
An oreo an orange
A Baby Ruth
Thrown ashore and
We would scramble
For such treasures
Eating dirt... and fruit
We'd never touch
At home

From concrete cliffs
Stretched along the shore
I learned to jump
Then dive and taste
My immortality
For in spite of
Sign and warnings
No one ever drowned

And once (just once)
A showboat came
Up river and tied up
At your side
Thrilling us all
With drama
And I remember
Buying popcorn
At intermission
From a beautiful girl
In black net hose
Who went on to play
The lead in all my
Fifth grade dreams

1975

Global Warning

Hey, it's getting hot around here
I mean, a nice hot day is a treat
But every day?
I can't keep ice in my drink
The squirrels are sweating
Birds pant but don't sing

Hey, it's getting hot around here
Do the politicians care?
Congress makes no progress
The White House residential
Could be presidential
And say, for instance
My fellow Americans
It's getting hot around here

Nooooooo… what we get
Are climate clowns who claim
It's just a phase, a blip
They know because they've been
Here for hundreds of years
Chopping off the head
Of every little chicken
Who looks up and says
Hey, things don't look good

I am not a nasty person
But I imagine them drowning
In a great swirl of
Seawater and sweat
So I sit and watch as
The mercury rises

My spirits fall, and at last,
I Google: *Ark Building for Idiots*

September 2012

The Intruder

Deep deep asleep
Hour of the wolf
Night of nighttime
Then narrowly awake
Wife's voice enters ear
Not…stop snoring
But
There's someone in the house
Anger wrestles with anxiety
Rise
Reluctant to respond
Step silently into slippered soles
Move from bed to door
And on to sound of
Slap slap slap
And there in lunar light
I see
In our dining room
Not a Dannamora dodger
No its Rocky Raccoon
Rolling end over end
40 oz. container of
Costco's Best Mixed Nuts
Toward the screen porch
Freedom and a feast
Just a swinging cat door away
I stomp my foot heroically
Rocky abandons nuts
Hits the great outdoors via cat door
Later by dawn's early light
I set nut container in cat door
And discover ah irony

It will not fit
I laugh and then imagine
Reservoir of raccoon regret
When the nuts will not pass

July 2016

The Faculty Meeting (collegium militari)

bent down behind my china shield
sunk deep within my mail
i see the snipers zip and zing
the ones who speak and fail

(machine gun laughter interlude)

i click the safety in my head
i will not think aloud
for i would rather sigh within
than bleed before this crowd

1974

Frank Stella's Darabjerd III

Mechanical peacock
Bred
In neon nest
You do not fly
Weighed down
I guess
By all that color

March 1976

The Third Law of Theodynamics

Expelled
From Eden's promise
we rolled the world
into The Wheel of Progress
backs bent, heads bowed
dig drill divide debate

but fossil fuels are dead… and dying
while heaven's gilded gift
warms us with her smile
and raised to holy howl
wind whispered spirit
calls us to a new beginning

October 1988

The Guitarist
for Tony

fingers fly,
bend and fret
but no worry
rising up are
trial balloons
note after note
melodic messages
shaping stories
some from memory
of teachers passed
most newly born
home made harmonies
rise then fade away
replaced again and again
feelings floating free
for…
music is not made
but found in and
liberated from
the deep heart's soul
… into the air…

June 2015

A Fracking Shame

To frack, or not to frack, that is the question:
Whether 'tis nobler in the eyes of the world to suffer
The stings and barbs of outrageous corporations
Or to take up pen against a flood of money
And by opposing silence them. To speak, to write
Not heeded; and by a word we say, stop
The drilling and the thousand unnatural shocks
That earth is heir to: 'tis a consummation
Decidedly to be needed. To speak, to write;
To march, perhaps be silent—yes, there's the challenge
For in that sleep of conscience, what death may come?

Late one night in 2015

Punkuation

Not tonight, I have my .

It's all gone, my dog – ate it.

If you _ you lose.

Look, it's an … of the sun!

I just had my first : oscopy

My sigmoidoscopy was a ; oscopy

Our kitchen looks much better with the new \

I believe Matthew, Luke, and John, but I ?

2014

Stoned

St. Stephen
had a reason
worth admiring
what's yours

March 1978

Thought For Food

couldn't sleep
got up
wrote short poem
thought
need a snack
balled up poem
ate it

2015

The Critics

One hot August night
Me and my friend Jim
Climbed through the
Men's room window of the
Park Theater (now defunct)
To see *Bitter Rice*
With Sylvana Mangano

We left the same way
One hour later
After
Too many subtitles
And
Too few tits

1975

Christmas Eve

on Christmas Eve
may the noise of
      our world
be broken
by a great burst
      of silence
releasing a shower
      of light
which covers us all
      in peace

Christmas 1990

Merry Crispness

Shepherds move flocks
To higher ground
Sheep smile while being
Sheered
Wise men wear shorts
And are frankly incensed
Mary and Joseph
Need no shelter
From the cold
And baby Jesus
Is completely unswaddled

What does this mean
It means
Or so it seems
That we have turned up
The heat
But we have not yet learned
To walk in the light

Fortunately
The light is still on

Jeff and Etta, 2013

A Christmas Cheer

With wise men lost
or deep in sleep
and shepherds tending
bar, not sheep,
it might seem odd
to celebrate a birth,
but we will push aside
the pine
and give the slip
to Santa,
to offer up a quiet cheer
for you, frail child,
Prince of Peace.
We're glad you're here.

Christmas 1975

Rock Music

sounds like
rolling stones

no wonder
the dead are grateful

2000

Paradise Remembered
song lyrics, sung to the tune of John Prine's Paradise

When I was child my family would travel
Down to the blue ocean to swim and have fun
There's a beautiful bay that's often remembered
With surf and white sand, and a whole lot of sun

So, daddy, please take me to Santa Monica Bay
To the beach and the water where we used to play
Well, I'm sorry my son, you're too late in askin'
The bay's all polluted and there's no fun today

Sometimes we'd surf on boards in the water
In the cold salty sea that sparkled and gleamed
Throw Frisbees and footballs and catch a few fish
Build castles of sand for all that we dreamed

So, daddy, please take me to Santa Monica Bay
To the beach and the water where we used to play
Well, I'm sorry my son, you're too late in askin'
The bay's all polluted and there's no fun today

Yes, oil was spilled from the world's biggest tanker
So the beach is a mess and you won't see a shark
The Hyperian Outfall let loose with its sewage
Now the surfers still surf, but they glow in the dark

So, daddy, please take me to Santa Monica Bay
To the beach and the water where we used to play
Well, I'm sorry my son, you're too late in askin'
The bay's all polluted and there's no fun today

When I die let my ashes float west on the water
Let my soul take its rest way down in the deep
I may be in heaven or I may be in hell
But at least I will have a pollution free sleep

So, daddy, please take me to Santa Monica Bay
To the beach and the water where we used to play
Well, I'm sorry my son, you're too late in askin'
The bay's all polluted and there's no fun today

March 1990

Ipso Facto

You want social stability?
We need economic viability
You want economic viability?
We need educational accessibility
You want educational accessibility?
We need generational responsibility
You want generational responsibility?
We need social stability

Summer 2012

The Ascension

James R. Hilty, Jr.
Preacher's kid extraordinaire
Tied his sister up
In a tree

And
On the next day
When she was found
Alive... unhurt... and well
Her father... Jim's too
Preached a sermon
On lost sheep
Which left us all
Up in the air

July 1975

Right Now

right now
near jackman maine
a squadron of geese
are flying by a radar tower
that sends signals
all the way to the pentagon
to warn us if
we're threatened
yet I feel fine just knowing
that the geese
are still flying

December 1974

Gawf
with apologies to E.B. Browning

How do I love thee? Let me count the strokes.
I love thee to the depth and breadth and height
My ball can reach when slicing out of sight.
For the end of rounds and ideal shots,
I love to the level of every player's
Most quiet need, by sun and failing light.
I love thee freely, as men strive for greens.
I love thee purely, as they turn from rough.
I love thee with the passion put to use
In my old clubs, and with my hacker's faith.
I love thee with a love I seemed to lose
With my last swing—I love thee with the pars,
Birdies, bogeys of all my life!
And if God choose
 I shall but play thee better after death.

June 2000

Imitation of Christ

Our lives take on
A cruciform
When
Living at cross purposes
We nail one another to
The tree of life

1978

Easter Saturday

Roll away the stone
Pressed tight
Against my heart

Reveal my empty
Tomb of faith

Touch me
Fill me
Raise me…
From my doubts
Again

1974

The Secret of the Golden Trout
with appreciation to Guatama Buddha, Jim Spaulding, and my Grandmother McClain

High above and far from frantic freeways
With dead air days and nervous neon nights
Granite guards stand watch
While piney preachers sign
With gnarly silent gestures

What message am I meant to see to hear
What truth to tuck away
Inside my pack my heart
That I should hike still farther
That I should climb still higher
Or
Is the word carried on the wind
By jay-scream or fly buzz
Or tucked inside a Tootsie Roll
Of marmot scat
Left everywhere for everyone
I do not know

But then at dusk
When shadows spread
And darkly dim my vision
I walk to the edge of Hidden Lake
And kneel and look
And suddenly
I see the truth of it all
C'est moi… it is me
I am in this place
This place is in me

I am mountain peak and deep valley
I am timid deer and bold chipmunk
I am willful wind and yielding yellow daisy
I am scudding cloud
Both black and white
I am flash of angry lightning and raging rain
Then sunshine smile
I am all of this and so much more
In this wild and beautiful place

No roaring jet above or
Careless camper down below
Can take away this truth
No camera click
Can freeze this piece of time
I am always in this place
This place is always in me

August 29, 1988 in the South Sierras

Last Standing Man
song lyrics

Out here on my back porch, wrapped up in the dark
My fires burnin' low, but I still have a spark
I'm still doin' the best, the best that I can
Just tryin' to be the last standin' man

Now I've had beginnings, and a whole lot of ends
Too many fixes, and not enough mends
But they helped me learn you must make amends
And to believe in your future, believe in your friends

So if you're out there wanderin', wrapped up in the dark
And your fires burnin' low, but you still have a spark
Keep doin' the best, the best that you can
And you could become the last standin' man

Just pick up your feet and lift up your chin
You might fall behind, but don't ever give in
Though the end of the road is far out of sight
You'll find your way home by your inner light

Trust in its warmth and its rock steady beam
It's what offers hope and allows you to dream
So keep keepin' on the best that you can
And you could become the last standin' man

September 2010

You've Got to Give to Get
song lyrics, for Etta

If I model for your role, will you model for mine
And if I bake the bread, will you buy the wine

If I look up to you, will you not look down on me
And if I let you trim my sails, will you let me set you free

> Spin world spin, I'm not quite finished yet
> For the lesson that I've learned
> You've got to give to get

If I pick you up, will you not let me down
And if I dry your tears, will you wipe away my frown

If you buy me bonds, I'll buy you stocks
And if I give you my keys, will you throw away your locks

> Spin world spin, I'm not quite finished yet
> For the lesson that I've learned
> You've got to give to get

If I plant the flowers, will you mow the lawn
And I'll make dinner at dusk, if you make you breakfast at dawn

If I give you my shirt, will you let me walk in your shoes
And if I help you write a love song, will you help me sing the blues

I'll live in your life, if you'll live in mine
Two lovers, one story, written line by line

Summer 2012

On Celebrating My 77th Birthday

I did not
die young
thank God
I was not
good

October 2016
Gualala, CA

ABOUT THE AUTHOR

McClain Jeffrey Moredock has worked as a farmhand, a lifeguard, a surveyor, a minister, a chaplain, a teacher, a coach, a head of school, and a chief operating officer. And, like many of his contemporaries, he retired at 65 and immediately began consulting. Five years later, weary of air travel and motel beds, he retired for good. Now 77 years old, he credits "whatever writing ability I have" to an unmedicated case of ADD and an inability to stop free-associating.

www.ingramcontent.com/pod-product-compliance
Lightning Source LLC
Chambersburg PA
CBHW061339040426
42444CB00011B/2991